CONTENTS

Page 20

Page 22

Page 28

Page 58

NFL Autograph Album

Jim Plunkett, Quarterback, Oakland Raiders

John Jefferson, Wide Receiver, San Diego Chargers

4

Wilbert Montgomery, Running Back, Philadelphia Eagles

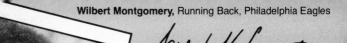

Randy Gradishar, Linebacker, Denver Broncos

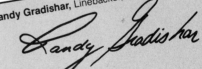

Billy Sims, Running Back, Detroit Lions

5

Earl Campbell

Earl Campbell, Running Back, Houston Oilers

Joe Theismann, Quarterback, Washington Redskins

Nolan Cromwell, Safety, Los Angeles Rams

Nolan Cromwell

Walter Payton

Walter Payton, Running Back, Chicago Bears

Art Still, Defensive End, Kansas City Chiefs

Arthur B. Still

Tony Dorsett, Running Back, Dallas Cowboys

Brian Sipe, Quarterback, Cleveland Browns

Marvin Powell, Tackle, New York Jets

Lynn Swann, Wide Receiver, Pittsburgh Steelers

Joe Cribbs, Running Back, Buffalo Bills

What's Your NFL I.Q.?

Here's a chance to find out how much you know about NFL players, coaches, and teams. Look on page 94 for the right answers.

1. Which former NFL quarterback is currently serving in the United States House of Representatives?
   a. Johnny Unitas
   b. John Brodie
   c. Jack Kemp

2. How many men make up an NFL officiating crew during the regular season?
   a. 11
   b. 7
   c. 5

3. The following NFL quarterbacks attended college in what state: Steve Bartkowski, Vince Evans, Pat Haden, Craig Morton, Jim Plunkett, Brian Sipe, and Jim Zorn?
   a. Alabama
   b. Rhode Island
   c. California

4. Which AFC team was NOT a charter member of the old American Football League?
   a. Baltimore Colts
   b. Houston Oilers
   c. Buffalo Bills

5. Which running back was the first in NFL history to gain more than 1,000 yards in each of his first four seasons?
   a. Jim Brown
   b. O.J. Simpson
   c. Tony Dorsett

6. Which man played more seasons, more games, and scored more points than any other man in NFL history?
   a. Jim Bakken
   b. George Blanda
   c. Bill Bergey

7. Which running back does NOT wear number 34?
   a. Billy Sims
   b. Walter Payton
   c. Earl Campbell

8. Which player is NOT a soccer-style kicker?
   a. Rick Danmeier
   b. Rafael Septien
   c. Tony Franklin

9. Which NFL player did NOT win the Heisman Trophy as a college junior?
   a. Billy Sims
   b. Jim Plunkett
   c. Archie Griffin

10. Which NFL player was a high hurdler for the U.S. Olympic team in 1976?
   a. Walter Payton
   b. Ottis Anderson
   c. James Owens

11. Which NFL head coach played a season in the National Basketball Association for the Lakers?
   a. Bud Grant
   b. Bum Phillips
   c. Don Shula

12. Which NFL quarterback did NOT play high school football in Shreveport, Louisiana?
   a. Terry Bradshaw
   b. Joe Ferguson
   c. Ron Jaworski

13. Which television announcer did NOT play in the NFL?
   a. Howard Cosell
   b. Frank Gifford
   c. Irv Cross

14. Where is the Pro Football Hall of Fame located?
   a. Albany, New York
   b. Green Bay, Wisconsin
   c. Canton, Ohio

15. Which running back was the first in NFL history to gain over 3,000 yards in his first two seasons?
   a. Earl Campbell
   b. Tony Dorsett
   c. Franco Harris

16. In what year was the National Football League organized?
   a. 1960
   b. 1939
   c. 1920

17. Which player has won the NFL most valuable player award?
   a. Roger Staubach
   b. John Stallworth
   c. Joe Greene

18. Which former running back is NOT a member of the Pro Football Hall of Fame?
   a. Jim Brown
   b. Jim Taylor
   c. O.J. Simpson

19. Which professional team is NOT a member of the NFL?
   a. Tampa Bay Rowdies
   b. Seattle Seahawks
   c. San Francisco 49ers

20. Which college has sent the most players to the NFL?
   a. USC
   b. Alabama
   c. Yale

21. Which member of the Pro Football Hall of Fame was known as "The Galloping Ghost" during his playing days?
   a. Horst Muhlmann
   b. Red Grange
   c. Gale Sayers

22. Which NFL team is the only one NOT displaying a logo on its helmet?
   a. Atlanta Falcons
   b. Buffalo Bills
   c. Cleveland Browns

23. What was the site of the first Super Bowl to be played indoors?
   a. Houston Astrodome
   b. Louisiana Superdome
   c. Seattle Kingdome

24. The NFL career record for consecutive games played is held by Jim Marshall of the Minnesota Vikings. How many?
   a. 1,230
   b. 282
   c. 714

A CARTOON HISTORY OF THE NFL

More than 60 years ago a group of men representing a handful of "town teams" from a few Midwestern cities met in Canton, Ohio to form what is now the National Football League.

Over the years the NFL has experienced growth and change, but along the way professional football developed into the number-one team sports attraction in America.

In the boom years of the 1920s, the NFL had as many as 22 teams. But in the 1930s, the number dwindled to only eight. More franchises were added prior to World War II, but the war forced membership down to eight teams again in 1943. Nevertheless, some of the greatest names in the game—Jim Thorpe, Red Grange, Bronko Nagurski, Johnny Blood (McNally), Don Hutson, and Sammy Baugh—played during pro football's first 25 years.

In the 1950s, with teams entering the NFL from the All-America Football Conference, pro football's popularity increased. Television helped bring the pro game and its brilliant individual stars to all parts of the country.

In 1960 the American Football League, began play. Ten years later the NFL changed its structure and absorbed 10 teams from the AFL into its new framework. The NFL split into two conferences—the American Football Conference and the National Football Conference—and with continued expansion in the 1970s, the NFL grew to 28 teams.

The Super Bowl, which began after the 1966 season as a title contest between the champions of the NFL and the AFL, has become one of the most important events in all of sports. The game now matches the winners of the AFC and the NFC to decide the NFL championship.

1920 A meeting is held in Ralph Hay's Hupmobile agency showroom in Canton, Ohio on September 17 to organize the American Professional Football Association. Among the participants are pro football pioneers George Halas and Jim Thorpe. Thorpe is elected president. The 13-team league plays its first season in 1921. The name of the league is changed to National Football League in 1922.

1923 Jim Thorpe leads the Oorang Indians team of Marion, Ohio. Players with the names of Arrowhead, Black Bear, Deerslayer, Xavier Downwind, Laughing Gas, Joe Little Twig, Red Fang, Stilwell Sanooke, Baptiste Thunder, Wrinkle Meat, Deadeye, and Lone Wolf are on the roster. Other legendary players such as Red Grange (Chicago Bears) and Johnny Blood (Milwaukee Badgers) begin their professional careers in 1925.

1932 A blizzard forces the NFL championship game between the Chicago Bears and the Portsmouth, Ohio, Spartans indoors. It is played on an 80-yard field. Chicago wins 9-0. The next season brings sweeping rule changes to the league. Goal posts are moved up to the goal lines, hashmarks are added to the field, and the football is slimmed down for easier passing. In 1934, the rules are further modified to permit passing from anywhere behind the line of scrimmage. The air game is born.

1939 The first Pro Bowl game is played. The NFL champion New York Giants defeat a team made up of NFL all-stars. The 1939 season also saw the first televised NFL game, the Brooklyn Dodgers against the Philadelphia Eagles, broadcast by NBC to the few television sets in use in New York City at the time. In 1940, in the most lopsided game ever played, the Chicago Bears (known as the "Monsters of the Midway") beat the Washington Redskins 73-0 for the NFL championship.

1943 It becomes a league rule that all players must wear helmets. Some didn't prior to the rule. Three years later, in 1946, a rival to the NFL, the All-America Football Conference (AAFC) begins play with eight teams: Brooklyn Dodgers, Buffalo Bisons, Chicago Rockets, Cleveland Browns, Los Angeles Dons, Miami Seahawks, New York Yankees, and San Francisco 49ers.

1948 Helmet logos make their debut. Fred Gehrke, a halfback with the Rams and a commercial artist, spends the offseason hand painting ram's horns on the team's helmets. Later that season, plastic helmets are banned and teams go back to using leather. In 1950, the NFL and the AAFC merge. The Baltimore Colts, San Francisco 49ers, and Cleveland Browns join the NFL from the rival league. In 1951, the Pro Bowl, dormant since 1942, is revived.

1958 A sudden death overtime period becomes necessary for the first time in an NFL championship game. Baltimore, with Johnny Unitas at quarterback, becomes the champion by beating the New York Giants 23-17 in what comes to be called the "greatest game ever played." The next season, another NFL rival, the American Football League, is formed. It begins play with eight teams in 1960, the same year that Pete Rozelle is named NFL commissioner.

1966 The AFL and NFL agree to a merger. Only preseason AFL-NFL games and the Super Bowl are to be played until the total merger is completed in 1970. In January, 1967, following the 1966 season, the Green Bay Packers beat the Kansas City Chiefs 35-10 in the first Super Bowl. On the last day of 1967, in an NFL championship game played in minus-13 degree weather, Green Bay defeats the Dallas Cowboys 21-17 on a one-yard quarterback sneak by Bart Starr.

1969 Quarterback Joe Namath "guarantees" victory for his underdog New York Jets in Super Bowl III—and produces the first Super Bowl victory for the AFL, 16-7 over Baltimore. The next year, teams begin play under the merger agreement. Previous NFL teams Baltimore, Cleveland, and Pittsburgh join the 10 AFL teams to form the American Football Conference. The remaining 13 NFL teams form the National Football Conference.

1971 In the longest game in NFL history, Miami defeats Kansas City 27-24 on Garo Yepremian's field goal in the AFC divisional playoffs. The game went into a second overtime period and lasted 82 minutes and 40 seconds in all. The next season's playoff thrill involved Miami again. The Dolphins put together the first perfect season in NFL history with a 17-0 record, including playoff games. Miami capped the season with a 14-7 victory over Washington in Super Bowl VII.

1973 O.J. Simpson of the Buffalo Bills rushes for a record 2,003 yards for the season. Behind the Bills' offensive line, the "Electric Company," "Juice" set five other NFL rushing records. By 1975, national attention shifts from Buffalo to Pittsburgh. In January 1975, the Steelers win Super Bowl IX 16-6 over the Vikings to capture their first championship since joining the NFL in 1933.

1978 The NFL goes to a 16-game schedule and a wild card round is added to the playoffs. Other changes include the addition of a seventh official, the side judge, and major rule changes that immediately begin to open up the passing game. At the end of the season, Minnesota quarterback Fran Tarkenton retires holding virtually all NFL career passing records.

1979 The Steelers, with superstars Terry Bradshaw, Franco Harris, John Stallworth, and Lynn Swann on offense, and the "Steel Curtain" defense featuring Joe Greene, Jack Ham, and Jack Lambert, become the team of the decade by winning Super Bowl XIV 31-19 over Los Angeles. It marks Pittsburgh's fourth Super Bowl victory (IX, X, XIII, and XIV), an unprecedented feat.

1980 After the Steelers' Super Bowl XIV victory, the Pro Bowl game is played in Honolulu, the first time it is played in a non-NFL city. In 1980, San Diego quarterback Dan Fouts breaks NFL records for single-season passing attempts (598), completions (348), and yardage (4,715). Three of his receivers, Kellen Winslow, John Jefferson, and Charlie Joiner, finished 1-2-3 in the AFC in catches. Each has more than 1,000 yards receiving. The Oakland Raiders become the first wild card team to win the Super Bowl by beating Philadelphia 31-10 in game XV.

MAZE OF TACKLERS

See if you can return the kickoff for a touchdown.

S T A R T

You've made it halfway! Continue at the top of the next page.

The solution to the maze
is on page 94.

The 25,000-Yard Club

One of the most exclusive statistical groups in the NFL is comprised of 14 pro quarterbacks who have passed for more than 25,000 yards. The members of the 25,000-yard club were each able to combine two important qualities: exceptional talent and durability.

Virtually every style of quarterbacking is represented in the 25,000-yard club. Fran Tarkenton of Minnesota and the New York Giants, the NFL's all-time passing yardage leader with 47,003 yards, is best remembered for his ability to scramble and throw on the run. The legendary Johnny Unitas of Baltimore and San Diego, the only other quarterback to gain 40,000 yards through the air, represented the classic passing style.

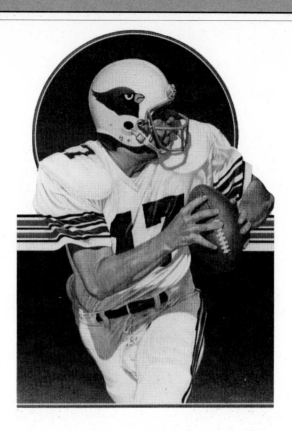

A pure, dropback "pocket passer," Jim Hart (above) moved into fifth place on the all-time NFL career passing yardage list in 1980. Hart is one of the oddities of the 25,000-yard club—he has reached 25,000 yards with just one team, the St. Louis Cardinals. Every other member except John Brodie (San Francisco) and Bob Griese (Miami, above left) played for at least two teams. Griese surpassed 25,000 yards in 1980.

The 25,000-Yard Club

Player	Years	Games	Att.	Comp.	Yards
Fran Tarkenton	18	246	6,467	3,686	47,003
Johnny Unitas	18	211	5,186	2,830	40,239
John Hadl	16	213	4,687	2,363	33,503
Sonny Jurgensen	18	218	4,262	2,433	32,224
Jim Hart	15	180	4,705	2,388	32,154
John Brodie	17	200	4,491	2,469	31,548
Norm Snead	16	178	4,353	2,276	30,797
Roman Gabriel	16	183	4,498	2,366	29,444
Len Dawson	19	211	3,741	2,136	28,711
Y.A. Tittle	15	178	3,817	2,118	28,339
Joe Namath	13	140	3,772	1,886	27,663
George Blanda	26	340	4,007	1,911	26,920
Bobby Layne	15	175	3,700	1,814	26,768
Bob Griese	14	161	3,429	1,926	25,092

George Blanda (left), Bobby Layne (right), and Y.A. Tittle (center): Blanda, who was also a placekicker, outlasted the others by more than a decade. Blanda played for Chicago, Baltimore, Houston, and Oakland; Layne for Chicago, the New York Bulldogs, Detroit, and Pittsburgh; and Tittle for Baltimore, San Francisco, and the New York Giants.

Another trio whose careers coincided was Sonny Jurgensen of Washington and Philadelphia (left), Johnny Unitas (top), and John Brodie (right). From the mid-1950s until the 1970s these men were among the most feared quarterbacks in the NFL and were picture passers almost without comparison.

A later generation: Len Dawson (left), Norm Snead (right), and John Hadl (middle). They rolled up passing yardage for several teams. Although Dawson is identified with the Chiefs, he also played for the Steelers and Browns. Hadl played for four teams (Chargers, Rams, Packers, and Oilers), while Snead spent time with five teams (Redskins, Eagles, Vikings, Giants, and 49ers).

Glamour, strength, and verve: Joe Namath (left), Roman Gabriel (top), and the king of the 25,000-yard club, Fran Tarkenton (right). Tarkenton finished his 18-year career at or near the top of every major NFL career passing category. Namath, who endured many injuries, played the fewest number of seasons (13, with the New York Jets and Los Angeles) of those in the club. Gabriel played for Los Angeles and Philadelphia.

There are seven men on a football field each week who try their best to be invisible. They are the officials and they are charged with keeping order in the game and making sure that each team plays by the rules. When you consider that the *Official NFL Rule Book* is 128 pages long and many of the rules are fairly complicated, you realize that those seven men have a very difficult job.

Jim Tunney, who has been an official in the NFL since 1960, says that the 105 officials the NFL employs go through a constant performance evaluation during the course of a season. As a referee, Tunney is charged with the "education program" of the officials in his crew.

"I see that the crew is together at least twenty-four hours before the game," he says. "We review the previous week's game film and discuss the weekly test that the league distributes to each official." On the field, Tunney (as the referee) is the man who will mark off and announce a penalty when either he or one of the other officials drops a flag. He will also settle any disagreements when two officials make contradicting calls on a play.

Who are these different officials and exactly what are their responsibilities dur-

There are three teams on the field at every NFL game: the offense, the defense, and the officials.

ing a game? Each has an area to cover and certain things he is supposed to watch for, which dictates where he positions himself.

The referee, in addition to his crew chief reponsibilities, is assigned to the quarterback and the other members of the backfield. He'll be watching for motion penalties in that area; for example, if a running back moves before the center snaps the ball, the referee will call a penalty.

The other six officials cover every area where a possible penalty could occur. The umpire stands near the linebackers (five yards from the line of scrimmage) and watches the line play, or the action "in the trenches"; the head linesman and the line judge straddle either side of the line of scrimmage near the sidelines. These three officials will watch for offensive and/or defensive holding and offsides. In addition, the head linesman is in charge of the chains and yardmarkers used for measuring first downs. The line judge also keeps the time of the game as a backup for the clock operator.

The back judge operates on the same side of the field as the line judge, but he is 17 yards downfield. The side judge is 17 yards downfield on the same side of the field as the head linesman. Both the back judge and side judge check for pass interference and any illegal offensive players downfield. The seventh official—the field judge—primarily observes the tight end. He stands 25 yards downfield from the line of scrimmage and also checks for pass interference. On punting downs he watches the punt returns, checks fair catches, and who retains possession if a kick is touched or fumbled.

Each seven-man crew remains together throughout the regular season. Officials work four preseason games, and 15 regular season games. Each crew gets one week off during the year. Tunney says that the league's constant evaluation of officials throughout the season really pays off during the championship playoffs. Only the top-rated crews get to work those games—including the most important one of the year—the Super Bowl.

Pro football officials, just like players, coaches, and trainers, arrive at the stadium on game day several hours before kickoff. The crew carries very little equipment with them—just their uniforms. They inspect the game balls, which are provided by the home team, for correct pressure and make sure that they are wiped clean of any foreign substances.

About 30 minutes before kickoff, the crew will check the condition of the field, the goal posts, the yardmarkers, and the chains. In addition, the umpire will check the linemen of both teams to make sure that the hand and arm wrappings many of them use are within the rules.

During the game, Tunney says, the officials try to understand that the players get caught up in the heat of action and may say things in a moment of anger that they probably don't mean.

"This is an emotional game," he emphasizes. "Players are going to get angry and complain when they feel a call is unfair and has gone against them. We'll tolerate some of that."

One way to stop it from getting out of hand is by penalizing a team 15 yards for unsportsmanlike conduct. That usually settles things. As a last resort the offical can eject a player from the game, and will do so automatically if the player bumps or touches any of the officials. The NFL rules call for such action when that happens.

Tunney says that one call that creates a lot of player complaints, and one of the toughest for officials to make, is pass interference.

"The players today are very quick and very clever," he says. "The most important things for any offical are to be in the best position to make the call, and not to anticipate. Sometimes a play develops and you can swear there will be interference; but then at the last second the defender avoids it. We can't drop that flag until it *happens*. In fact, we have a slogan or a rule, 'Let it happen, don't anticipate.'"

What do NFL officals do when they're not working pro games? Well, unlike players, coaches, and trainers, during the week they return to regular, outside-football jobs. For example, Tunney was a high school administrator and principal for 17 years before he started his own public speaking organization.

"Our officials come from all areas of private business," he says. "We have many teachers and school administrators; we also have bankers and insurance salesmen. We have a pharmacist, a podiatrist, even a man who owns his own lumber yard."

Tunney emphasizes it would be misleading to say that because these men hold other full-time jobs the league doesn't employ professional and experi-

(Right) Before games, officials check players' wrappings and the air pressure of the game's 13 footballs. (Below) Each member of an NFL officiating crew has a specific field position and area of responsibility.

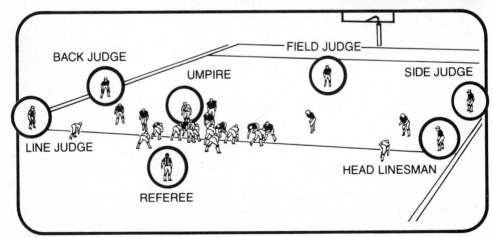

BACK JUDGE

FIELD JUDGE

UMPIRE

SIDE JUDGE

LINE JUDGE

HEAD LINESMAN

REFEREE

enced officials.

"No official gets to work in the NFL without having a lot of prior experience," he says. "Every one of them has between fifteen and eighteen years experience at the college level. We get the majority of our men from the major college conferences, such as the Big Ten and Pac Ten."

Officals are paid different amounts for each type of game they work; for working in the preseason, they are paid $300, and in the regular season, $325-$800, depending on seniority. Those officials who are graded best and are chosen to work postseason games get more money— $2,000 for playoff games, $3,000 for the Super Bowl, and $1,000 for the Pro Bowl.

Officials travel all over the country each week of the season. They don't receive any special consideration, such as the league assigning many Midwestern games to an official who, for instance, lives in Chicago. In fact, Tunney, who lives in Northern California, says, "At times I believe the league thinks I really live in New Jersey because of all the East Coast games I keep getting."

But after two decades as an NFL official, Tunney still has the enthusiasm of a rookie. It doesn't take him long to say why.

"I enjoy working with people who are the best in the world at what they do," he emphasizes. "People like Walter Payton and Dan Fouts. That's what keeps me interested, excited, and coming back for more."

Officials don't see all of the action during a game because they must watch only one part of each play.

NFL PHOTO QUIZ

1

These objects familiar to NFL fans have been photographed from some very different angles. Can you guess what they are? The answers are on the Answers page.

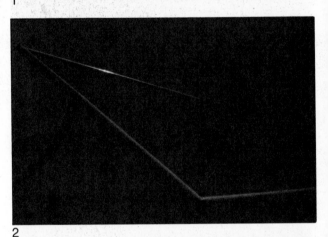

2

3

4

5

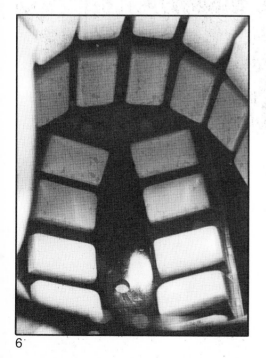

6

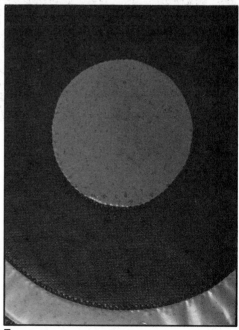

7

WHAT'S YOUR CALL?

Officiating an NFL game can be very tricky. It demands a complete knowledge of the rules, quick thinking, and outstanding judgment. Below are five situations that actually occurred in NFL games. Pretend you are the official and see if you can make the correct call. The answers are on the next page. Good luck!

1. New Orleans has the ball, second down and 10 yards to go for a first down from its own 8 yard line. The Saints' quarterback takes the snap and rolls out to the right. He crosses the scrimmage line and goes to the 11 yard line, where he throws a forward pass. As the Saints' receiver reaches up for the ball on his 30 yard line, a Rams defensive back pushes him out of the way, intercepts the ball, and runs for a touchdown. What would you rule?

a. *Defensive pass interference — Saints' ball on their 30 yard line.*

b. *Rams touchdown.*

c. *Saints' ball, third and 14 from their 6 yard line.*

d. *Replay the down, since both teams committed fouls on the play.*

2. In a game at New York, Dallas leads the Giants by two points with a minute left to play. The Giants line up for a field goal from Dallas's 12 yard line. The kicker kicks the ball with his right foot. A Cowboys lineman blocks the ball with his chest. The ball bounces back to the kicker's left, and he kicks it again, this time with his left foot. The ball goes over the crossbar. What would you rule?

a. *Field goal.*

b. *Touchback.*

c. *Penalize the Giants 15 yards from the spot of the snap.*

d. *Penalize the Giants 15 yards from the spot of the second kick.*

3. On fourth down and 10 yards to go for a first down from their own 30 yard line, the Cardinals punt. The kick is partially blocked by a Redskins lineman, who then runs into the punter. The ball bounces behind the line of scrimmage, where a St. Louis player picks it up and throws a forward pass to a teammate, who catches the ball 20 yards downfield and runs for a score. What would you rule?

a. *Touchdown.*

b. *Replay the down.*

c. *Penalize Washington five yards for running into the kicker, which gives the Cardinals a first down at their 35.*

d. *Redskins' ball, first and 10 on St. Louis's 30 yard line.*

4. It's San Diego's ball, third and 18 from its own 4 yard line. The quarterback throws a pass from his own end zone. The pass is batted down by a Houston lineman. The ball goes right back into

the hands of the quarterback, who is still standing in the end zone. He flips the ball forward to one of his backs, who is also in the end zone. The back is immediately tackled, fumbles, and a Houston player recovers the ball in the end zone. What would you rule?

a. *San Diego's ball, fourth down and 18 on its 4 yard line.*

b. *San Diego's ball, fourth down and 20 on its 2 yard line.*

c. *Touchdown for Houston.*

d. *Safety against San Diego.*

5. On a kickoff to start the game a Rams player catches the ball on his 10 yard line and runs toward his left on a criss-cross pattern. He hands the ball forward from his 15 yard line to a teammate, who takes the ball on his 16 yard line. The second ball carrier is tackled immediately and fumbles the ball, which is recovered by Atlanta on the 16 yard line. The Falcons player then runs for a touchdown. What would you rule?

a. *Touchdown.*

b. *Atlanta's ball, first down and 10 from its own 16.*

c. *Rams' ball, first down and 10 from the Atlanta 16 yard line.*

d. *Rams' ball, first down and 10 from the Atlanta 10 yard line.*

ANSWERS

1.b. It is a touchdown and not pass interference. Pass interference rules do not apply to an illegal pass unless it is the second pass from behind the scrimmage line. This was an illegal pass as the passer threw the ball from beyond the scrimmage line. Illegal passes may be intercepted.

2.b. The kicker kicked a loose ball, which is a foul. The ball went over the end line after it crossed the crossbar and therefore was a touchback, since the kicking team put the ball out of the opponent's end zone. Had the kicker regained full possession of the ball, he would have been permitted to dropkick it. If the defending team, Dallas, had not declined the penalty, then the Giants would have been penalized 15 yards. But Dallas wisely chose not to give the Giants another chance for a field goal.

3.a. A team is allowed to throw one pass from behind the line of scrimmage during a play from scrimmage. As long as it was the first forward pass from behind the line, as it was in this case, it is legal—even though a kick had been attempted first. A player may run into a kicker if he touches the kicked ball in flight as he tried to block the kick. That is not a penalty. It would have been a penalty if he hadn't touched the kick in flight and run into the kicker.

4.a. This is considered a second forward pass from behind the scrimmage line, which is an illegal pass and results in a loss of down from the previous spot. An illegal forward pass caught by an offensive player is dead immediately. When this particular pass was caught, the play was over. The subsequent fumble and recovery didn't count.

5.d. It is an illegal pass since it is handed forward. It is a five-yard penalty from the spot of the forward handoff. The ball is dead when handed forward and possessed by a teammate. Nothing else can happen after that as far as that play is concerned.

FOOTBALL FOR LAUGHS

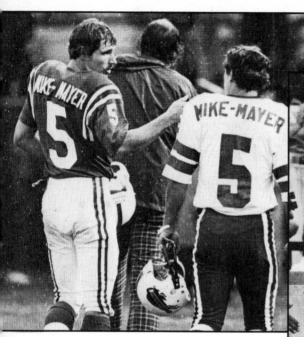

If a picture is worth 1,000 words, then a caption on a funny picture makes it worth even more. Try your hand at writing some funny lines to go with these photos.

See our example at right.

I've heard of trap plays but this is ridiculous!

Making it Official

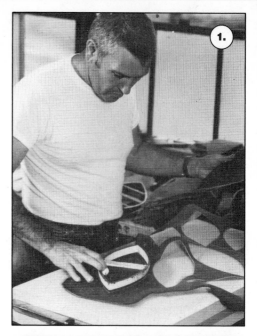

The most important item for an NFL game is not the field, or a kicking tee, or even goal posts. It is a football. It sounds obvious, but it's something few people think about.

In fact, did you know that although a football is called a "pigskin" it's actually made from cowhide?

Come along, then, on a tour of the Wilson factory in Ada, Ohio, and see how official NFL footballs are made.

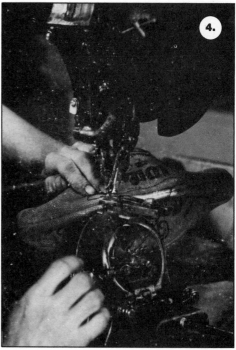

1. A section of cowhide is cut into the shape of a football.
2. The leather inner panels, also made from cowhide, are sewn together, inside out, on a heavy duty lockstitch machine.
3. The inner panels are turned right-side out. This prepares the ball for insertion of the rubber bladder, which will hold the air in and keep the ball inflated.
4. A machine punches out holes to prepare the ball for threading.
5. The outer coverings of the footballs await the insertion of rubber bladders.

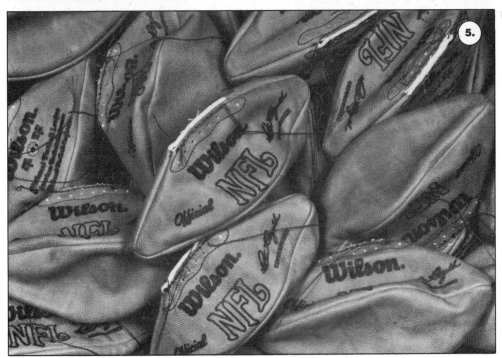

6. The last step in putting the bladder inside the ball involves careful stitching around the outer inflating valve.

7. Each ball is laced by hand.

8. The football assembly line. Before the ball is packaged it must be placed in a mold and inflated to 80 pounds of pressure. This will straighten the seams and match the ends of the ball where the seams meet. The ball is then buffed to bring out its natural texture and feel. At this step, it is deflated to the playing pressure of 13 pounds.

9. The finished product; the football is now ready for NFL action.

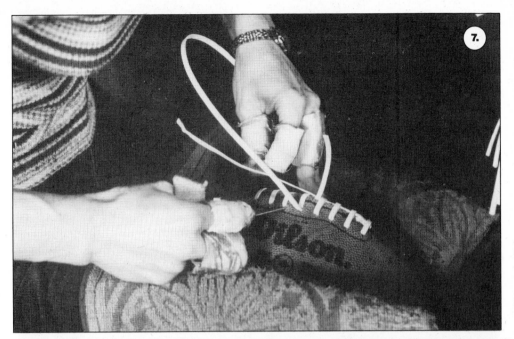

The NFL: 28 Teams, 28 Stories

The teams of the National Football League annually captivate the imaginations of millions of devoted fans—from the day preseason training camps open to the final Sunday more than six months later when the AFC-NFC Pro Bowl is played. In between, the 28 NFL teams stage a dramatic quest for the Super Bowl championship.

After a series of rookie camps, free agent tryouts, and veterans' mini-camps in the spring and early summer, NFL teams officially begin their preseason training in July. The first few weeks of the camp are devoted primarily to conditioning drills, team meetings, and intrasquad scrimmages.

Each team also plays a minimum of four preseason games. The preseason schedule opens with the annual Hall of Fame Game, which coincides with the induction of new members into the Pro Football Hall of Fame. The game is played in Canton, Ohio, the birthplace of the NFL and the home of the Hall of Fame.

The first weekend in September annually signals the onset of the 16-game regular season, which continues into December.

The league is divided into two conferences (American and National) of three divisions each (East, Central, and West). Each team plays every other team in its own division twice, and rounds out its schedule with games against teams from other divisions in both conferences.

When the regular season concludes, another "season" begins: the playoffs. Each division winner, along with the two teams from each conference with the next-best records (wild card teams), qualify to compete for the conference championships.

The first week of the playoffs involves games between the wild card teams. The winners advance to the second round with the three divisional champions. The excitement continues to build the following week when the conference championship games are played.

When the two conference champions have been decided, they meet in the Super Bowl, which has become one of the most important events in all of sports.

The NFL's season finale comes after the Super Bowl when a team of all-stars from the AFC meets its counterpart from the NFC in the AFC-NFC Pro Bowl.

ATLANTA
FALCONS

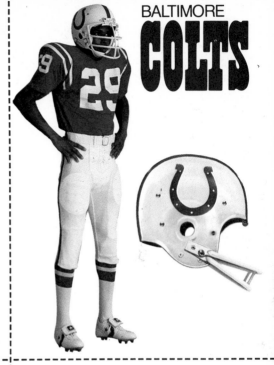

BALTIMORE
COLTS

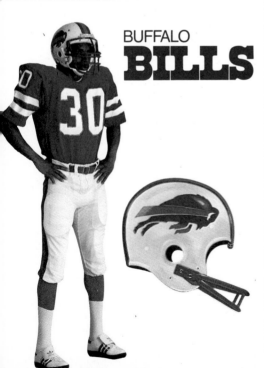

BUFFALO
BILLS

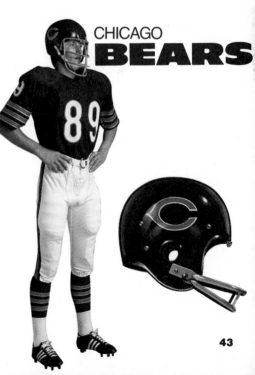

CHICAGO
BEARS

BALTIMORE COLTS — AFC EAST

The Colts joined the NFL in 1953 and quickly became a power. End Gino Marchetti and tackle Gene (Big Daddy) Lipscomb were two of the team's early defensive stars. With offensive greats such as quarterback Johnny Unitas, running back Lenny Moore, and wide receiver Raymond Berry also on hand, Baltimore won the 1958 NFL championship by beating the New York Giants in sudden death overtime. Many people consider that 23-17 victory to be the greatest game ever played in the NFL. The Colts repeated as champions in 1959. They also won the NFL title in 1968, but were upset by the AFL's New York Jets in Super Bowl III. In 1970 the Colts returned to the Super Bowl and defeated Dallas 16-13 to win the world championship. Unitas, selected as the greatest quarterback in NFL history, is one of six Colts in the Pro Football Hall of Fame.

ATLANTA FALCONS — NFC WEST

In 1980 Atlanta won the NFC Western Division championship with a best ever record of 12-4. It was the first title of any kind for the Falcons, who entered the NFL as an expansion team in 1966. Tommy Nobis, an All-America linebacker from the University of Texas, began the Falcons' tradition when he became the first player chosen in the 1966 college draft. Nobis didn't disappoint the Falcons; he enjoyed an outstanding career and played in three AFC-NFC Pro Bowls. Quarterback Steve Bartkowski, another number-one pick by the Falcons, was the initial player chosen in the 1975 draft. He has proceeded to set most of the Falcons' significant single-season and career passing records. Another great NFL quarterback, Hall of Famer Norm Van Brocklin, coached Atlanta from 1968-1974.

CHICAGO BEARS — NFC CENTRAL

Since becoming part of the original NFL in 1920, the Bears have forged a glorious heritage that includes six NFL championships and 19 members in the Pro Football Hall of Fame—more than any other team. Legendary owner George Halas has been with the Bears since their inception, first as a player in the early 1920s, and then, for 40 years as the team's coach. As coach, he compiled pro football's best won-lost record (320-147-30 in regular season games). Since the 1920s and 1930s, when Red Grange became the NFL's first real superstar, Chicago has been known for its great running backs. Others include Bronko Nagurski, George McAfee, Rick Casares, Gale Sayers, and Walter Payton. Another great Bear was Pro Football Hall of Fame linebacker Dick Butkus, who was named all-NFL eight times.

BUFFALO BILLS — AFC EAST

Buffalo was one of the original members of the American Football League. When the AFL and NFL merged in 1970, the Bills joined the American Football Conference's Eastern Division. In the mid-1960s, the Bills were a dominant team. Led by quarterback Jack Kemp, they won back-to-back AFL championships in 1964-65. In 1969 the Bills opened the door to an exciting new era when they named Heisman Trophy winner O.J. Simpson as the number-one choice in the college draft. Simpson developed into one of the best running backs the NFL has ever seen. In 1973 he became the first player to rush for more than 2,000 yards in a season (with 2,003). Three years later he set an NFL single-game rushing record (since broken) of 273 yards. In 1980, the Bills won the AFC Eastern Division title for the first time.

CINCINNATI
BENGALS

CLEVELAND
BROWNS

DALLAS
COWBOYS

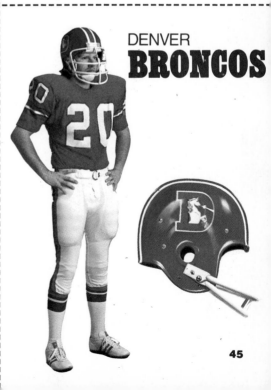

DENVER
BRONCOS

45

CLEVELAND BROWNS   AFC CENTRAL

Some of the greatest names in NFL history have played for the Cleveland Browns. The list includes quarterback Otto Graham, tackle and kicker Lou Groza, and running back Jim Brown. The Browns entered the NFL in 1950, and head coach Paul Brown immediately led the team to the NFL championship. Cleveland appeared in the NFL championship game the next five years, winning the title in 1954 and 1955. Jim Brown played his entire career with Cleveland and set the all-time NFL career rushing record of 12,312 yards. He led Cleveland to another NFL crown in 1964. Cleveland, along with the Baltimore Colts and Pittsburgh Steelers, became part of the American Football Conference when the NFL merged with the AFL in 1970. The Browns won AFC Central titles in 1971 and 1980.

CINCINNATI BENGALS   AFC CENTRAL

Cincinnati first made its appearance in the AFL in 1968 and finished that initial season with an unimposing 3-11 record. One bright spot that year was the play of running back Paul Robinson, who won the AFC rushing title with 1,023 yards and was named AFC rookie of the year. But the Bengals rapidly developed into a strong contender and captured AFC Central Division championships in 1970 and 1973. The man primarily responsible for the Bengals' quick development was Paul Brown, the former Cleveland Browns head coach who came out of retirement to become the Bengals' first head coach and general manager. Another former Cleveland coach, Forrest Gregg, was named head coach at Cincinnati in 1980. Some of the top players in the Bengals' brief history include quarterback Ken Anderson, wide receiver Issac Curtis, and safety Tom Casanova.

DENVER BRONCOS   AFC WEST

The Broncos were one of the charter members of the American Football League. The franchise struggled during the 1960s, but head coach John Ralston, who was hired in 1972, led the team to its first winning season in 1973 with a 7-5-2 record. Red Miller took over as coach in 1977, a season that turned into a high water mark for the Broncos. With Craig Morton at quarterback, and a defense—"The Orange Crush"—sparked by linebacker Randy Gradishar and end Lyle Alzado, Denver finished 12-2 in the regular season. The Broncos defeated Oakland 20-17 to win their first AFC championship, but lost 27-10 to the Dallas Cowboys in Super Bowl XII. Running backs Floyd Little and Otis Armstrong and wide receiver Lionel Taylor are some of the top players who have worn Denver uniforms.

DALLAS COWBOYS   NFC EAST

The Dallas Cowboys have achieved remarkable success since joining the NFL in 1960. Beginning in 1966, the Cowboys posted 15 consecutive winning seasons. During that period the team won 11 division or conference titles, appeared in the playoffs 14 times, and played in five Super Bowls, winning games VI and XII. Their regular season record during that span: 159-55-2. The team's great record is a tribute to head coach Tom Landry, who has led the Cowboys since their very first season in the league. Defensive stars such as Pro Football Hall of Fame tackle Bob Lilly, linebacker Lee Roy Jordan, and safety Cliff Harris have complemented offensive standouts such as quarterback Roger Staubach, running backs Calvin Hill and Tony Dorsett, and wide receivers Bob Hayes and Drew Pearson.

DETROIT
LIONS

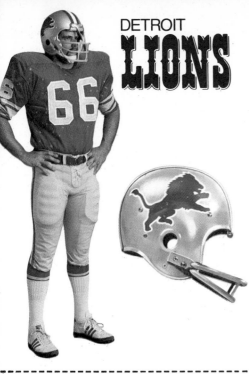

GREEN BAY
PACKERS

HOUSTON
OILERS

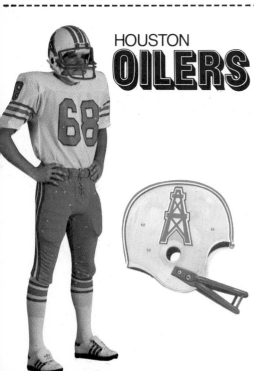

KANSAS CITY
chiefs

GREEN BAY PACKERS   NFC CENTRAL

The Green Bay Packers, one of the oldest franchises in the NFL, have the unique status of being a community-owned corporation. The Packers got their start in 1919 when Earl (Curly) Lambeau talked his employers, the Indian Packing Company of Green Bay, Wisconsin, into spending $500 for football equipment. Led by Johnny Blood (McNally), a Pro Football Hall of Fame halfback, the Packers won consecutive NFL championships between 1929-1931. Under legendary head coach Vince Lombardi, the Packers dominated the league in the early and mid 1960s, winning NFL titles in 1961, 1962, 1965, 1966, and 1967. The 1966 and 1967 teams, featuring quarterback Bart Starr, and linebacker Ray Nitschke, won Super Bowls I and II against AFL champions Kansas City and Oakland, respectively.

DETROIT LIONS   NFC CENTRAL

Almost a half century ago, the Lions began a long and successful association with the Detroit area. The franchise began as the Portsmouth, Ohio, Spartans in 1930, but moved to Detroit four years later and became the Lions. In 1935, the team won its first NFL championship. Detroit was a dominant team in the 1950s, winning back-to-back world titles in 1952 and 1953. Stars during that era included Pro Football Hall of Famers Bobby Layne and Jack Christiansen, as well as Doak Walker, who ran 67 yards for the decisive touchdown in the 17-7 victory over Cleveland in the 1952 title game. In 1957, Tobin Rote quarterbacked the Lions to a 59-14 rout of the Browns for the Lions' last NFL championship. In 1975 the Lions moved from Tiger Stadium to the Pontiac Silverdome, an indoor arena with over 80,000 seats.

KANSAS CITY CHIEFS   AFC WEST

One of the six original members of the American Football League was the Dallas Texans, who were owned by millionaire oilman Lamar Hunt, the man responsible for the creation of the league. The team experienced attendance problems in 1961 and 1962, so in 1963 Hunt moved the franchise to Kansas City and renamed the club the Chiefs. Head coach Hank Stram, who was hired when the team was formed in 1960, molded the Chiefs into a championship squad later in the decade. Featuring stars such as quarterback Len Dawson, running back Mike Garrett, defensive tackle Buck Buchanan, and linebacker Bobby Bell, the Chiefs won the AFL title in 1966 and represented the league in Super Bowl I. Kansas City lost that game 35-10 to the powerful Green Bay Packers. Three years later the Chiefs returned to the Super Bowl—Game IV—and earned a 23-7 victory over the Minnesota Vikings.

HOUSTON OILERS   AFC CENTRAL

The Houston Oilers joined the American Football League in 1960 and immediately proved they belonged by winning the league's first two championships. The star of those early teams was quarterback and placekicker George Blanda, formerly with the Chicago Bears, who had been talked out of retirement. The Oilers also won AFL Eastern Division titles in 1962 and 1967, but then the team slipped. Seven years after the AFL-NFL merger the Oilers once again developed into a strong playoff contender. Under head coach Bum Phillips they qualified for the playoffs in 1978, 1979, and 1980. Running back Earl Campbell, who was a rookie in 1978, led the NFL in rushing in each of his first three seasons, and had a spectacular total of 1,934 yards in 1980.

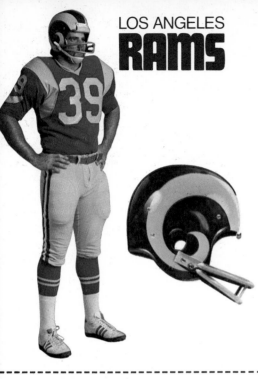

LOS ANGELES
RAMS

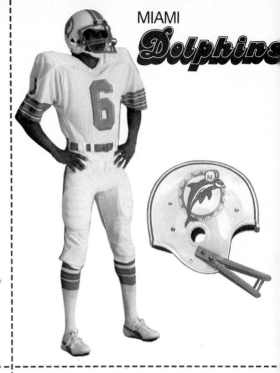

MIAMI
Dolphins

MINNESOTA
VIKINGS

NEW ENGLAND
PATRIOTS

MIAMI DOLPHINS — AFC EAST

In 1966, the Miami Dolphins began play in the American Football League. Just five years later, under new head coach Don Shula, the Dolphins finished second in the AFC East and made the playoffs. In four of the next five years, Miami finished first in the AFC East. The Dolphins appeared in their first Super Bowl in 1971 but lost 24-3 to Dallas. The following season, in Super Bowl VII, the Dolphins capped the first perfect season (17-0) in NFL history with a 14-7 victory over Washington. The Dolphins came back the next year to win Super Bowl VIII. Central to the Dolphins' great success in those years was an outstanding backfield sparked by quarterback Bob Griese and running backs Larry Csonka, Mercury Morris, and Jim Kiick, and a group called the "No-Name Defense," led by linebacker Nick Buoniconti.

LOS ANGELES RAMS — NFC WEST

The Cleveland Rams joined the NFL in 1937 and achieved their greatest moments in 1945 when rookie quarterback Bob Waterfield led the team to a 9-1 record and the league championship. The following season the team moved to Los Angeles, and soon enjoyed success on the West Coast. The Rams won Western Division championships in 1949, 1950, and 1951. The 1951 Rams defeated Cleveland 24-17 in the NFL title game on a 73-yard scoring pass from Norm Van Brocklin to Tom Fears. In 1955, new head coach Sid Gillman led the Rams into the championship game again, but this time they lost to the Browns. The Rams won the Coastal Division under head coach George Allen in 1967 and 1969, and from 1973-79 the team won seven straight Western Division titles. The Rams appeared in Super Bowl XIV, but lost to Pittsburgh.

NEW ENGLAND PATRIOTS — AFC EAST

The Boston Patriots began play in 1960 as the eighth team in the American Football League. Three years later, under head coach Mike Holovak, the Patriots won the AFL's Eastern Division, but lost 51-10 to San Diego in the championship game. Quarterback Babe Parilli and wide receiver-kicker Gino Cappelletti were early stars for the Patriots. The team struggled from 1964 to 1975, posting only two winning seasons. But in 1976, led by daring quarterback Steve Grogan and a strong 3-4 defense, the Patriots posted an 11-3 record and made the playoffs. They lost to eventual Super Bowl champion Oakland in the final 39 seconds of a first-round game. In 1971 the club moved from Boston to Foxboro and changed its name to the New England Patriots.

MINNESOTA VIKINGS — NFC CENTRAL

Minnesota was awarded an NFL franchise in 1961 and in 1968 the Vikings won their first NFC Central Division championship. The 1969 Vikings went a step further by winning the NFL title, but lost to the Kansas City Chiefs in Super Bowl IV. Those Vikings' teams featured one of the top defensive lines in history. Known as the "Purple People Eaters," Alan Page, Gary Larsen, Carl Eller, and Jim Marshall terrorized offenses around the NFL. The Vikings' quarterback in their early years, Fran Tarkenton, was traded to the New York Giants in 1967, but he returned to Minnesota in 1972 and went on to become the all-time leading passer in NFL history. Tarkenton and the Vikings competed in three additional Super Bowls (VIII, IX, and XI) without success. Since 1967, Minnesota's head coach has been Bud Grant, who has led the team to 11 NFC Central titles.

NEW ORLEANS
SAINTS

NEW YORK
GIANTS

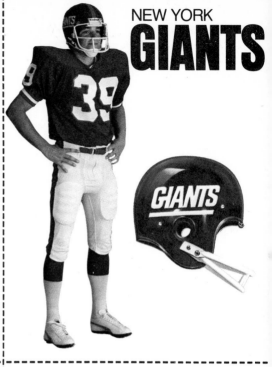

NEW YORK
JETS

OAKLAND
RAIDERS

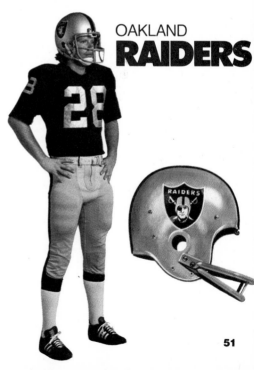

NEW YORK GIANTS   NFC EAST

The New York Giants have a rich history, dating from the team's first preseason game in 1925 when players such as Century Milstead, Hinkey Haines, and the legendary Jim Thorpe lined up to play Ducky Pond's All Stars. Over the years the Giants have won 14 conference and four NFL championships, the most recent in 1963. Steve Owen, who coached the Giants from 1931-1953 compiled an impressive record of 151-100-17 and was elected to the Pro Football Hall of Fame. Among the many other Giants who have been elected to the Hall of Fame are owner Tim Mara, center Mel Hein, tackle Roosevelt Brown, halfback-flanker Frank Gifford, defensive end Andy Robustelli, quarterback Y.A. Tittle, and safety Emlen Tunnell. In 1976 the team moved to their new location, Giants Stadium in East Rutherford, New Jersey.

NEW ORLEANS SAINTS   NFC WEST

New Orleans joined the NFL in 1967. Although the Saints have never enjoyed a winning season, they have contributed their share of upsets, thrills, and great players to the NFL. The Saints' best performance came in 1979, when they finished 8-8 and wound up second in the NFC Western Division. Among the Saints' many outstanding performers are placekicker Tom Dempsey, who set an NFL record with a 63-yard field goal in 1970; quarterback Archie Manning, who holds virtually all of the club's passing records; and wide receiver Danny Abramowicz, who began his NFL record string of 105 consecutive games with at least one pass reception (since broken) with the Saints. Following the 1980 season, New Orleans hired former Houston Oilers head coach Bum Phillips to build the club into a contender.

OAKLAND RAIDERS   AFC WEST

Since 1963, just three years after the Raiders began play in the American Football League, the team has compiled a stunning record of 179-68-11, the best in pro football during that period. Sixteen consecutive winning seasons, 11 playoff appearances, and three trips to the Super Bowl are among the highlights. The Raiders lost to Green Bay in Super Bowl II, but have since won Super Bowls XI (over Minnesota) and XV (over Philadelphia). Oakland boasts a tradition of outstanding quarterbacks. Daryle Lamonica, Ken Stabler, and Jim Plunkett each led the team to a Super Bowl appearance. Wide receiver Fred Biletnikoff, center Jim Otto (the first Raider to be named to the Pro Football Hall of Fame), quarterback-placekicker George Blanda, cornerback Willie Brown, guard Gene Upshaw, and running back Marv Hubbard have all contributed to the Raiders' huge success over the years.

NEW YORK JETS   AFC EAST

The New York Jets were originally called the Titans when they joined the American Football League in 1960; the name was changed in 1963. Following their first winning season ever under head coach Weeb Ewbank in 1967, the Jets went all the way to the top the next year. After arriving in Miami to prepare for Super Bowl III, brash, young quarterback Joe Namath "guaranteed" a victory over the NFL champion Baltimore Colts. With the help of running back Matt Snell, wide receiver George Sauer, and a staunch defense, Namath made good on his promise and led the Jets to a 16-7 upset over the heavily favored Colts. Namath was a great quarterback but knee injuries hampered his career. When he was signed by Los Angeles in 1977, the Jets began a rebuilding program under new head coach Walt Michaels.

PHILADELPHIA
EAGLES

PITTSBURGH
Steelers

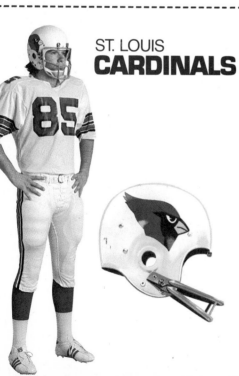

ST. LOUIS
CARDINALS

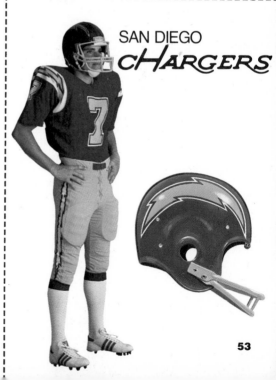

SAN DIEGO
CHARGERS

PITTSBURGH STEELERS   AFC CENTRAL

The Steelers were founded in 1933 by Art Rooney. A long, often frustrating cycle of building, rebuilding, and more rebuilding finally paid dividends in 1974 when the Steelers won their first NFL championship by defeating Minnesota 16-6 in Super Bowl IX. That victory signaled the beginning of a Pittsburgh dynasty. The Steelers went on to dominate the NFL in the late 1970s. They won the Super Bowl an unprecedented four times: 1974, 1975, 1978, and 1979. Head coach Chuck Noll, hired in 1969, constructed a balanced team. Quarterback Terry Bradshaw, running back Franco Harris, and wide receiver Lynn Swann keyed a productive offense, while the "Steel Curtain" defense, featuring linemen Joe Greene, L.C. Greenwood, and Dwight White, and linebackers Jack Ham and Jack Lambert, was one of the most feared in the NFL.

PHILADELPHIA EAGLES   NFC EAST

The Eagles came into existence in 1933, but the team enjoyed little success until the 1940s. Then, powered by the running of Steve Van Buren, Philadelphia won back-to-back NFL championships in 1948 and 1949. In 1960 an Eagles team built around quarterback Norm Van Brocklin, wide receivers Tommy McDonald and Pete Retzlaff, and iron man Chuck Bednarik, who played both offense and defense, defeated Green Bay 17-13 to win their third NFL title. The Eagles fell upon hard times throughout most of the 1960s and 1970s. Dick Vermeil was hired as head coach in 1976 and quarterback Ron Jaworski, running back Wilbert Montgomery, linebacker Bill Bergey, and wide receiver Harold Carmichael helped lead a resurgence that carried the Eagles to the NFC championship and Super Bowl XV in 1980.

SAN DIEGO CHARGERS   AFC WEST

The Chargers entered the American Football League as a charter member in 1960 and played one year in Los Angeles before moving to San Diego. The early Chargers, under head coach Sid Gillman, were one of the most exciting teams in football and had an explosive offense that featured quarterback John Hadl, running backs Keith Lincoln and Paul Lowe, and wide receiver Lance Alworth. During the AFL's first six seasons, the Chargers were Western Division champions five times and won the AFL title in 1963. After a down period, head coach Don Coryell was hired in 1978 and installed the most prolific passing offense the NFL has ever seen. The Chargers won AFC Western Division titles in 1979 and again in 1980, when quarterback Dan Fouts broke his own NFL record by passing for 4,715 yards.

ST. LOUIS CARDINALS   NFC EAST

The Cardinals, one of the NFL's oldest clubs, began as a neighborhood team on the south side of Chicago in 1899. When the NFL was founded in 1920, the team joined as the Racine Cardinals (named for a street in Chicago). They became the Chicago Cardinals in 1922 and three years later won the NFL championship. Some of the greatest Cardinals teams played in the late 1940s. Led by running back Charley Trippi and quarterback Paul Christman, the 1947 Cardinals had a record of 9-3 and defeated Philadelphia 28-21 to win the NFL championship. In 1960 the Cardinals moved to St. Louis, but didn't enjoy much success until the mid 1970s, when head coach Don Coryell led the team to NFC Eastern Division titles in 1974 and 1975. Some of the top players from those teams included quarterback Jim Hart, running back Terry Metcalf, and wide receiver Mel Gray.

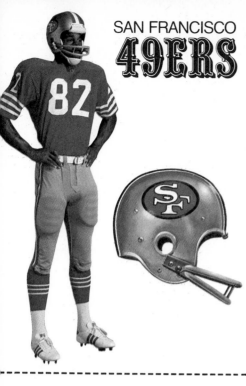

SAN FRANCISCO
49ERS

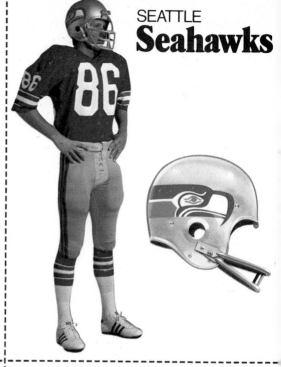

SEATTLE
Seahawks

TAMPA BAY
BUCCANEERS

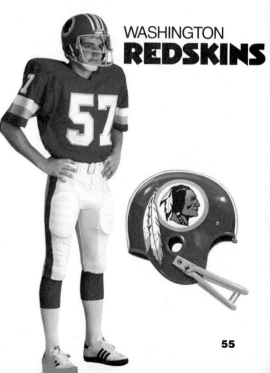

WASHINGTON
REDSKINS

SEATTLE SEAHAWKS   AFC WEST

One of the two newest franchises in the NFL, Seattle began play in 1976 in the Kingdome, an indoor stadium that seats 65,000. Initially the Seahawks struggled, winning just two games in their first season. Things got better in 1977, when they won five games and finished fourth in the five-team AFC West. In 1978, with quarterback Jim Zorn running an explosive passing offense, the Seahawks finished with a surprising 9-7 record and narrowly missed the playoffs. Seattle duplicated its 9-7 record the following year and again just missed a berth in the playoffs, with running back Sherman Smith and wide receivers Steve Largent and Sam McCullum complementing Zorn in the Seahawks' offense.

SAN FRANCISCO 49ERS   NFC WEST

The 49ers were founded in 1946 and began play under head coach Lawrence (Buck) Shaw in the All-America Football Conference. After finishing second to the Cleveland Browns for four years, the 49ers joined the NFL in 1950. San Francisco featured a "Million Dollar Backfield" in the early 1950s that included three future Pro Football Hall of Famers: running backs Joe Perry and Hugh McElhenny, and quarterback Y.A. Tittle. Another member of that team, Leo Nomellini, who played tackle on offense and defense, was also elected to the Hall of Fame. The 49ers struggled in the 1960s, but under head coach Dick Nolan the team became a contender again in the early seventies. Led by quarterback John Brodie, the 49ers won NFC West championships in 1970, 1971, and 1972.

WASHINGTON REDSKINS   NFC EAST

After playing in Boston for five years, the Redskins moved to Washington in 1937. That same year they signed a rookie quarterback from Texas Christian University named Sammy Baugh. It turned out to be a wise move, as Baugh threw three touchdown passes to help Washington defeat the Chicago Bears 28-21 in the NFL championship game. Baugh helped the Redskins dominate the Eastern Division in the early 1940s and his passing, kicking, and play at defensive back made him one of the greatest all-around players in the history of pro football. The Redskins were one of the NFL's top teams in the early 1970s. Led by head coach George Allen, they won the NFC championship in 1972 but lost Super Bowl VII in Los Angeles to the undefeated Miami Dolphins, 14-7.

TAMPA BAY BUCCANEERS   NFC CENTRAL

Tampa Bay joined the NFL in 1976 and lost all 14 of its games that season. By losing its first 12 games in the 1977 season the Buccaneers set a new NFL record for most consecutive losses (26). They finally broke the streak with a victory over New Orleans in the Louisiana Superdome, and closed the 1977 season by beating the Cardinals at home. The team improved to 5-11 in 1978, but no one was ready for what happened in 1979. Head coach John McKay led the team to a 10-6 record and the NFC Central Division championship. The upstart Buccaneers, with a tough young defense anchored by the Selmon brothers, Lee Roy and Dewey, and exciting quarterback Doug Williams, defeated Philadelphia in an NFC Divisional Playoff before losing 9-0 to Los Angeles in the NFC Championship Game.

SUPER BOWL RINGS

I Green Bay	II Green Bay	III New York Jets
IV Kansas City	V Baltimore	VI Dallas
VII Miami	VIII Miami	IX Pittsburgh
X Pittsburgh	XI Oakland	XII Dallas
XIII Pittsburgh	XIV Pittsburgh	XV Oakland

15 SUPER GAMES

It has become the single most publicized and anticipated sports day in America— Super Sunday and the Super Bowl. The old AFL-NFL rivalry has diminished, but each year football fans everywhere eagerly await the game and all the excitement that goes along with it.

The first Super Bowl was going to settle all the arguments caused by the question: Could the best team in the seven-year-old American Football League compete with the best team in the National Football League, which had been in existence for 46 years? Unfortunately for the AFL's Kansas City Chiefs (in Super Bowl I) and the Oakland Raiders (in game II), the NFL representative was the Green Bay Packers. Under Coach Vince Lombardi the Packers had become the dominant team of the 1960s—five times the NFL champion.

The Packers were led by quarterback Bart Starr, who ran their ball-control of-

fense with precision. In both games Starr was named the most valuable player. His pin-point passing and expert play-calling enabled Green Bay to move the ball consistently and to score both on long drives and with the big play. The Packers' defense, with all-pros at several positions, came up with its own big plays in both games, including cornerback Herb Adderley's 60-yard touchdown run with an intercepted pass in game II. By winning back-to-back Super Bowls, 35-10 over Kansas City and 33-14 over Oakland, the Packers set the standards by which other great teams would be judged.

Super Bowl III will forever be remembered as the game quarterback Joe Namath "guaranteed" the New York Jets would win. The NFL's Baltimore Colts were nearly three-touchdown favorites and most football people said that they would easily defeat the Jets. Namath was brash and confident, and a few days before the game he made his famous "We'll win, I guarantee it," statement. And Joe delivered, with some help from running back Matt Snell, kicker Jim Turner, and the Colts themselves, who at times played as if they couldn't believe what was happening to them. AFL fans all over the country rejoiced at the Jets' 16-7 victory, because it meant that the AFL could beat the NFL, that it had arrived.

Not everyone, however, was convinced that the AFL had reached "equality" with the NFL. Many NFL fans said that the Jets had been lucky. But after game IV even these critics were silenced. The Chiefs avenged their Super Bowl I loss by thoroughly dominating the Minnesota Vikings offensively and defensively in a 23-7 victory. Kansas City used a variety of offensive formations to confuse Minnesota. On defense, the Chiefs' pass rush harassed Vikings quarterback Joe Kapp into three interceptions. Now not even NFL die-hards could deny that the AFL had arrived.

In 1970 the two leagues merged and from then on the Super Bowl has been between two *conference* champions playing under the banner of one league—the NFL. Game V was actually between two "old" NFL teams because the AFC representative was the Baltimore Colts, who with two other teams (the Cleveland Browns and the Pittsburgh Steelers), had moved over to join the 10 AFL clubs to make up the new 13-team American Conference. Their opponent was the Dallas Cowboys.

The game was a comedy of errors (four lost fumbles and six interceptions). The Colts scored on a 75-yard pass after it had bounced off two players. Despite the miscues and unusual play, the game had an exciting finish. Rookie Jim O'Brien kicked a 32-yard field goal with five seconds left to give Baltimore a 16-13 win.

Dallas got a chance to erase their last-second loss the next year in Super Bowl VI. With quarterback Roger Staubach and running back Duane Thomas leading the way, the offense had little trouble putting 24 points on the board against a Miami Dolphins defense that was quick, but small. The Dallas defense, led by tackle Bob Lilly and safety Cornell Green, was ferocious all day. The Dolphins managed only a field goal, the first time a Super Bowl team had been held without a touchdown.

A pattern was beginning to emerge: teams that had lost in their first Super

Vince Lombardi gets a Super Bowl II victory ride.

Bowl appearance were coming back to win the next time they played in the game. That had been the case for the Chiefs, Colts, and Cowboys; now in Game VII Miami got a chance to follow suit. For the Dolphins the Super Bowl VII victory was even sweeter: it gave them a perfect 17-0 record for the year, the only undefeated, untied season in NFL history.

Miami was basically the same team Dallas had so soundly beaten the year before. But coach Don Shula had filled some weak spots, and Bob Griese, Larry Csonka, and the "No-Name Defense" had a year's more experience. It showed in games VII and VIII.

In game VII Miami beat Washington's veteran "Over the Hill Gang," and did it more convincingly than the 14-7 score indicated. The next year the Dolphins reached their peak. Griese and Co. became a scoring machine—a methodical, conservative, ball-control team. The defense played better as a *whole* unit than any defense in recent seasons. They beat Minnesota 24-7, and football people were beginning to call Miami the Packers of the 1970s—they were the first team since Green Bay to win back-to-back Super Bowls.

The dynasty was short-lived, however. Over the horizon was another AFC team waiting to step into the spotlight—the Pittsburgh Steelers. In Super Bowl IX the Steelers faced Minnesota, which was out to avenge two Super Bowl losses. Unfortunately for the Vikings, the Steelers and their "Steel Curtain" defense were on the verge of becoming a true dynasty that would rule the NFL to the end of the decade.

The names of the Steelers' stars have become very familiar to all fans by now: Terry Bradshaw, Franco Harris, Lynn Swann, and John Stallworth on offense; Joe Greene, Jack Lambert, and Jack Ham on defense.

In game IX, Pittsburgh held the Minnesota offense without a touchdown despite all of quarterback Fran Tarkenton's scrambling and won 16-6. In game X against the Cowboys, Bradshaw hooked up with Lynn Swann four times for a total of 161 yards, including a 64-yard touchdown bomb for the winning score. Staubach battled the Steelers right to the end, but the Pittsburgh defense made one last big play, intercepting a fourth down pass in the end zone in the final seconds to save a 21-17 win.

The Oakland Raiders returned to the Super Bowl in 1977 after years of falling one step short. As had been the case in three previous games, the unfortunate victim was Minnesota.

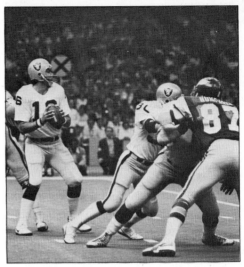

Jim Plunkett helped Oakland win Super Bowl XV.

Oakland won Super Bowl XI 32-14 and they won it with a big and powerful offensive line that completely dominated the line of scrimmage. Quarterback Ken Stabler and his offense produced 429 yards, and scored three touchdowns and two field goals. The defense let Tarkenton complete his short passes all day, but they gave up only two scores.

Game XII was almost a replay of game VI; a Dallas team with excellent offensive and defensive balance overwhelmed an AFC team with some glaring weaknesses. This time it was the Denver Broncos that were no match for the Dallas machine.

The Denver offense went nowhere. Harvey Martin, Randy White, and the rest of Dallas's "Doomsday" defense forced seven first-half turnovers, recovering three fumbles and intercepting Broncos quarterback Craig Morton four times. Meanwhile, Dallas wide receiver Butch Johnson made a spectacular dive across the goal line to make a fingertip catch of a

45-yard pass from Staubach, and the Cowboys went on to win by 17 points, 27-10.

The late 1970s saw the return of the Pittsburgh Steelers to the Super Bowl, ready to prove to the football world that *they* were the team of the decade. Game XIII was the first Super Bowl rematch ever. This time, the Cowboys and Steelers put on another classic battle as they had in Game X.

Bradshaw had an outstanding game— four touchdown passes for 318 yards; Staubach was nearly his equal with three touchdowns and 228 yards. But, once again, the Cowboys came up short at the end. They had cut an 18-point deficit in the fourth quarter to four points. But when the Cowboys' second consecutive onside kick was recovered by the Steelers with 22 seconds left, Pittsburgh had won 35-31 to become the first three-time Super Bowl champions.

The Steelers returned to the title game the next year. Their opponent in game XIV

was the Los Angeles Rams—led by an inexperienced quarterback named Vince Ferragamo. Ferragamo surprised the Steelers (and all the experts) by passing and play-calling like a seasoned veteran. But while driving for the potential winning score late in the fourth quarter, he made one mistake. Linebacker Jack Lambert intercepted an errant pass and the Steelers preserved an unprecedented *fourth* Super Bowl championship. They won 31-19.

Oakland became the new AFC champion and faced the Philadelphia Eagles in Game XV. Oakland quarterback Jim Plunkett climaxed his amazing 1980 comeback with an excellent game, expertly guiding the offense and throwing three touchdown passes. The standout on Oakland's defense was linebacker Rod Martin, who made life miserable for quarterback Ron Jaworski by intercepting three of his passes. With the 27-10 victory, the Raiders became the first wild card team ever to win a Super Bowl.

Name Droppers

NFL Cities

1. Atlanta
2. Baltimore
3. Buffalo
4. Chicago
5. Cincinnati
6. Cleveland
7. Dallas

8. Denver
9. Detroit
10. Green Bay
11. Houston
12. Kansas City
13. Los Angeles
14. Miami

15. Minnesota
16. New England
17. New Orleans
18. New York (Giants)
19. New York (Jets)
20. Oakland
21. Philadelphia

22. Pittsburgh
23. St. Louis
24. San Diego
25. San Francisco
26. Seattle
27. Tampa Bay
28. Washington

```
O L A F F U B L E R O M I T L A B
N E W E N G L A N D H A H F C K W
H D T K R O Y W E N E P O T I G G
P K T A M P A B A Y G D U R N C L
H M A D C I U J K S A M S H C M Z
G S A N D I E G O L H O T R I V M
R G B A S D H G L I C I O N N P S
U C R L F A E A T S U I N U N S E
B A M E L Y S T I A M E E G A I L
S A B V E B K C R A S T L D T U E
T T Z E L N N F I O R S T E I O G
T L K L C A B M T T I T T N U L N
I A M C R O I A Q N Y T A V E T A
P N G F P N E W Y O R K E E W S S
X T N E W O R L E A N S S R K G O
O A K L A N D P X C H I C A G O L
S L N Y R A I H P L E D A L I H P
```

Try these two all-pro word search puzzles. The left one contains the names of cities with NFL teams, the right one contains the 28 team nicknames. Can you find them? The answers are in the Answers section.

NFL Team Nicknames

1. Bears
2. Bengals
3. Bills
4. Broncos
5. Browns
6. Buccaneers
7. Cardinals
8. Chargers
9. Chiefs
10. Colts
11. Cowboys
12. Dolphins
13. Eagles
14. Falcons
15. 49ers
16. Giants
17. Jets
18. Lions
19. Oilers
20. Packers
21. Patriots
22. Raiders
23. Rams
24. Redskins
25. Saints
26. Seahawks
27. Steelers
28. Vikings

```
H S C H A R G E R S O Z A K C G S
S F N P B C S S P B G S L L I B Y
O N G O O R N N V M L L F R H Y O
C T Y L C I T X W I E T B E P L B
N P T C H L M L O O A M U X I S W
O S A P S L A N I D R A C S K H O
R F L T T G S F S W P B C W T V C
B O X D R A I D E R S W A R Y E U
D S E S O I K M F S T H N G Z I J
K T P N Z J O F C R A S E L G A E
C N L I S T M T L E R A E U M B K
P A C K E R S K S L E H R P E N S
K I G S E J S F Q I T G S N R O T
J G S D K B R S H O Y E G K A G N
U S T E E L E R S L I A S C M Y I
V T J R M P 9 R G F L M N T S T A
E S R A E B 4 T R S V I K I N G S
```

The Men Upstairs

NFL teams have coaches in the press box who analyze opponents and call plays.

Have you ever wondered about the coaches on the sideline who wear headsets: what they're saying, what they're listening to, and who they're speaking with? Well, they're getting suggestions and advice on offensive and defensive plays. Their sources of information are the press box coaches, who have a much better view of what is happening on the field than anyone on the sidelines.

The idea of a team putting members of its coaching staff in the press box to get a better overview of the game is not a recent one. Some teams began experimenting with field-to-press box communications as early as the 1950s; however, the results were sometimes less than productive.

Jack Faulkner, assistant general manager of the Los Angeles Rams, remembers an incident back in the mid-1950s when the team tried to institute some field-to-press box communications.

"We were experimenting with walkie-talkies one time in Chicago," he recalls. "Things were going along fine for awhile until midway in the first half we started getting all this police stuff over the air. It seems the Chicago Police Department had some cops in the stadium with walkie-talkies and they started using our frequency. For the rest of the game, no matter what we did, we had police interrupting our discussions."

Today NFL teams do not have to worry about outside interference from either the local police or the opposing team. All teams have special communication setups between the sidelines and the area of the press box reserved especially for them. Their headset-to-headset systems have advanced to the point where the coaches upstairs can speak directly with the team's head coach, the men in charge of the offense and defense, and even a key player who is not on the field at the moment, such as the quarterback or defensive captain. The coaches and players can hold one-to-one conversations or they can all speak with each other simultaneously.

Pro teams employ anywhere from three to five assistant coaches in the press box during a game. The press box people keep charts and give advice to those on the sidelines, and in some cases even call the offensive or defensive plays directly from upstairs. Many head coaches are their own offensive or defensive coordinators, which means they concentrate on calling the plays for one particular unit. They leave the running of the other squad entirely up to that squad's coordinator, whether he is on the sidelines or up in the press box.

Philadelphia head coach Dick Vermeil is the Eagles' offensive coordinator; that means he calls the offensive signals and leaves all the defensive play calling to the team's defensive coordinator, Marion Campbell. During 1980, the Eagles used five men in the press box during the game, three for offense and two for defense. One of the offensive coaches was Sid Gillman, a former head coach of the Rams, Chargers, and Oilers. He is generally credited with having one of the great offensive coaching minds in the history of the game.

For the past two seasons it was Gillman's job to monitor the opponent's defense and to concentrate primarily on the ways the Eagles' quarterbacks could take advantage of any weaknesses.

"Since Dick was the offensive coordi-

nator, we didn't actually call any plays from upstairs, but we were constantly feeding him information on how the other team's defense was reacting to our play selection," Gillman says. "You get a much better overview from the press box and with all twenty-two players spread out in front of you, you can really spot weaknesses a lot better than you can from the sidelines."

Each NFL team keeps what is called a "down and distance chart," which is a computer printout of what a team likes to do in various situations. For example, the Eagles' chart lists what one of their opponents, such as Oakland, likes to do (run or pass) on first down and 10 on their own 20 yard line, or second and 15 from their opponent's 35 yard line, or first and goal from the 4 yard line, and so on. The charts are made up during the week prior to the game and are based on the viewing of the game films each team must provide to its upcoming opponent.

The press box coaches will keep these charts in front of them during a game and at the same time will begin new ones to see if the opponent is actually doing what the computer and coaches had predicted it would.

"It is the coach's job," Gillman says, "to see if the other team is following what we call their 'normal tendencies,' and if not, to suggest adjustments in the game plan so that we could deal effectively with whatever 'new' things they are doing."

At halftime, the offensive and defensive coaches come down from the press box to meet with their respective coordinators and players in the locker room. Gillman says the head coach might even ask for some new plays to run in the second half

65

Coaches talk to the press box through headsets.

based on what the opponent has done.

"He [Vermeil] may say, 'Give me five runs and five passes to use this half,'" Gillman explains. "It depends on how we're doing. But even if we've been very successful the first half, you don't go back up there and relax for the rest of the game.

"You keep the charts, keep making suggestions, because the game can change suddenly and you're not up there to be a spectator. And the more the guys down on the field use your suggestions, the more you feel a part of the game."

Faulkner spent several seasons working in the press box for the Rams before becoming assistant general manager in 1980. He says there are advantages to coaching from high above the field.

"One big advantage is that it is easier to stay calm because there is a lot less confusion," says Faulkner. "Down on the field, with guys yelling and players coming in and out of the game, the coaches get emotionally involved. It's easy to lose your bearings.

"Up in the press box, with everything out in front of you and with the physical detachment from the field, you're in a better position to see things and give advice," he continues. "Of course you have to be careful not to give too much advice. As long as the guys down on the field are calling the plays, they're in control. But I always felt I was contributing a lot, and I think it's actually the best place to watch the game."

One coach who obviously agrees with Faulkner is Woody Widenhofer, who is Pittsburgh's defensive coordinator. Widenhofer calls all the defensive signals from his spot in the press box.

"I think it's very important for the coordinator to be in the press box," Widenhofer says. "From upstairs you can remain a little aloof, keep your poise, and have complete control of the situation."

Widenhofer is hooked up to two of his assistants on the sideline. One of them— assistant head coach George Perles— will relay Widenhofer's play selection to Steelers linebacker Jack Lambert, who will call the play in the huddle on the field. Since the defense usually breaks and lines up before the offense, Widenhofer must call his play based on what he *thinks* the opponent's offense will do on the next down.

"The first thing I check after a play is the down and distance chart," Widenhofer says. "Then I check formations and field tendencies and call the play based on those factors. One major advantage from upstairs is that it's much easier to keep

From the press box, coaches can see plays developing better than they can standing on the sideline.

track of substitutions. They play a key role in signal calling. For example, a team may be in a passing situation based on down and distance and field tendency. But, they've put two tight ends in the game. Well, that looks like a running formation, so the play I call has to definitely take that into account. And from upstairs I can see all of that a lot clearer than from the side-lines."

Widenhofer says that Steelers head coach Chuck Noll, who is also the offensive coordinator, has very little to do with the defense during the game.

"Chuck stands next to my defensive coaches when we're on defense, but I never communicate directly with him," he says. "He lets me and my staff run the defense completely. Of course, during the week before the game he meets with the defensive staff and he knows what we're

going to do on defense on game day."

Widenhofer stays upstairs until the gun goes off at halftime and then heads right to the locker room to meet with his assistants and players to discuss the first half's mistakes and successes.

"At halftime we try to find out *why* things are or are not working," he explains. "I think it's very important for the players to know why we're doing something instead of expecting them to follow orders blindly.

"As for making adjustments, we do that as the game progresses. We can't afford to wait until halftime. That's why being in the press box is so important. With all the charts in front of me, and the playing field wide open below, it's much easier to call checks and audibles [changes] to counter unexpected formations. From up there you can see it all."

OFFBEAT IN THE OFFSEASON

For six months each year more than 1,260 men who play professional football share a common lifestyle. Every player's routine is basically identical from July until February: training camp, practice at least five days a week, plenty of team meetings, and the games.

When the season ends, however, these men go their separate ways, not only geographically, but in their offseason jobs, careers, and activities as well. And, many NFL players spend their six free months pursuing some pretty interesting and strange careers; some even use them as the first step in planning for their lives after they stop playing football.

Dave Stalls has spent his recent offseasons involved in something his fellow players must find *very* strange — Stalls studies sharks. That kind of activity makes his playing defensive end for Tampa Bay seem like a rather mild and tame profession by comparison. But Dave doesn't do his studying up close; he and the sharks are separated by the aquarium walls at California State University at Long Beach, where Dave is pursuing a master's degree in marine biology.

He spends hours studying the behavior patterns of sharks — specifically the bull shark, a six-to-seven foot, very aggressive member of the species. Dave feels his area of study can be very useful in the future.

"If we could learn to read shark behavior, we might be able to interpret their moods and predict when they'll attack," he says. "After 'Jaws,' people started to believe that sharks had it in for humans, that they had some kind of 'personal feelings' against us."

Dave says that just isn't the case, and he hopes that his thesis on the communicative behavior of the bull shark will help clear up some of the misunderstandings.

Of course some people who know him think it's *his* behavior that needs to be studied because he also plans some scuba diving to observe the sharks at close range. "Some people think I'm crazy," he admits.

Many other players have used their off-season activities as a starting point for careers after their football days are over.

Tom Pridemore is one such player. An interest in politics and encouragement by West Virginia Governor Jay Rockefeller persuaded the Atlanta Falcons' safety to run for a seat in his native West Virginia's state legislature. And, despite his opponents' claims that he couldn't devote enough time to politics, Pridemore was elected to one of the three vacant seats in the 1980 election.

Since the legislature meets for only 60 days each year, Pridemore sees no conflict with his playing career. In fact, he pledged during the campaign to make himself more available to the people he would represent than the other candidates.

"They kept asking how I could repre-

sent the people and be gone part of the year in Atlanta," says Pridemore, whose teammates now call him "Senator." "But I'm sure that somebody who works at another job twelve months a year won't be as available as much as I am. And I'm setting up an office that will be open all year."

After performing in front of television cameras for six months, some players find they like it so much they want more of it. Steelers quarterback Terry Bradshaw, who in past summers has recorded country and western songs and performed in Las Vegas, spent the 1981 off-season making a pilot television show called "The Stockers," about stock car racers.

Detroit tight end David Hill has done just the opposite of Bradshaw. He switched from performing in front of the camera to working *behind* it. Hill works for a Detroit television station as a cameraman

69

on news and other live shows. Television runs in Hill's family; his brother Jim, a former pro cornerback, now works as a full-time sportscaster in Los Angeles.

After half a year running around on grass and turf, many players find they like it so much they want to stay in "touch with the land" for the other six months, too. The NFL has an entire farming community; cattle farmer Charlie Hall (Cleveland), cotton farmer Steve Freeman (Buffalo), horse breeder Mel Blount (Pittsburgh), chicken farmers John and Charley Hannah (New England, Tampa Bay), soybean and corn farmer Nolan Cromwell (Los Angeles), and pecan farmer John James (Atlanta).

And then there is Buffalo's Conrad Dobler, who retreats each year to Laramie, Wyoming, to work indoors *and* outdoors. Dobler operates his own 25,000 watt FM radio station in Laramie, and

spends his spare time participating in things such as the log-throwing event in the June Woodchoppers Jamboree in the Wyoming town of Encampment.

"You've got to throw an eight-to-nine-foot log that weighs eighty to ninety pounds and flip it so it walks end over end," Dobler says.

Last but not least, there's Denver guard Tom Glassic. While Dobler plays with 90-pound logs, Glassic plays with tiny toy soldiers. Now that might sound like a silly activity for a football player, but Glassic does more than just play with toy soldiers.

He is a full-time financial partner in a unique Denver store called "Old Soldiers Home." It specializes in selling toy soldiers from almost every historical era, uniforms to go with them, and many books on military history so one can read all about the various battles the soldiers fought in.

Glassic says there are a lot of people

like him, people who have both an interest in collecting toy soldiers and in studying the military history behind them.

"There are three types of collectors and collecting," he says. "There are those who collect antique metal toy soldiers, many of which aren't available anymore.

"Then there are those who are into 'war gaming' with toy soldiers, actually recreating historic battles using models of the surrounding countryside, with trees, lakes, and rivers, so that the entire battlefield is duplicated.

"Finally, there are the 'connoisseur collectors' who take unpainted figures, buy uniforms, and take them home to outfit them for whatever historical period they choose."

Glassic says he is into all three types, but enjoys war games the most. He pours over military history books and learns as much about particular battles as he can.

Then he will set up an entire battlefield and go at it with someone else's "army."

"I don't think it's any fun having soldiers in your collection if you don't know what those soldiers actually did in battle," he says.

Glassic's collection numbers between 4,000 and 5,000 pieces, and he has put part of it into the store he helped to start. He also continues to add to his collection by "getting first choice" when the store acquires new pieces. His dream is to devote all his time to the store and military history research.

How did his fellow players react when they learned of his unusual interest?

"Well, at first some of them couldn't figure out my passion for this," he says. "But now I've gotten three or four other guys on the team as interested as I am. We're always war-gaming when we're not playing football."

The Man Behind the Tape

One of the most important members of any pro football organization never plays a down and never diagrams an offensive or defensive play. He works as hard as anyone on the team during preparations before each week's game; yet on game day players, coaches, and fans would just as soon not see him on the field at all. Who is this rather unknown mystery man? He's the team trainer.

One former all-pro football player once said: "If the head coach is a football team's father, then the trainer is the team's mother."

The trainer is the first link between the players and the rest of the organization — coaching staff, physicians, and the front office. "We're sometimes a den mother, sometimes an ambulance driver," says Jerry Rhea, head trainer for the Atlanta Falcons since 1970. "A trainer is charged with the first-line maintenance of the athlete. He is the first person the athlete sees when he is sick or hurt."

The trainer's main job is to keep all the players healthy, and to get those who have been injured back into action as soon as possible. The job is a full-time one. From the time training camp opens in early July until a team's last game of the season, most work long, hard days. And in recent years, the job's responsibilities have increased so much that many trainers work almost full-time schedules during the offseason.

"Sports medicine is expanding so quickly, this really has become a full-time, year-round job," says Atlanta's Rhea. "It used to be you could go home in January and come back in June. Now you have to be here practically every day just to keep up with all the changes."

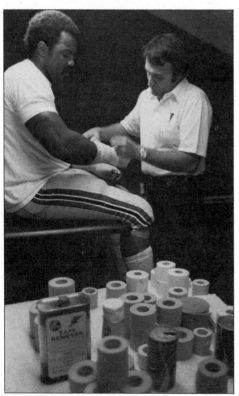

Atlanta trainer Jerry Rhea works on pregame taping.

And it's obvious football is benefiting from the extra effort. "The surgeons are better, and our treatment and rehabilitation programs are so much more advanced, that it is rare to have a player's career ended today by, say, a knee injury, the injury everyone still fears the most," Rhea says.

When it comes to dealing with injuries, the trainer and his staff—most NFL teams have one or two full-time assistants to the head man—work very closely with the team physician. All NFL teams have at least one full-time physician on staff. He is available for consultation most days during the week and is present at every game. If a player is injured, it is the trainer and the team physician who work out a schedule and rehabilitation program for the player to follow. And it is they who monitor the player's progress and make the final decision as to when he will be able to return to action.

Trainers usually have no formal medical training or background. However, they all know emergency first-aid techniques and how to operate emergency equipment. This, of course, is in addition to knowing the best way to treat sprains, pulled muscles, and bumps and bruises with ice, pressure bandages, and other techniques.

Leo Murphy has been with the Cleveland Browns since 1950. "The best way to learn this job is by on-the-job training," he says. "The key to this job is to get along with people. Outside of their wives, we spend more time with the players than anyone else. We're someone they can talk to, complain to, and get help from."

With his three decades of experience, Murphy emphasizes that the most impor-

tant thing in his profession is to recognize each player as an individual. "Each will react differently to an injury," he says, "or the frustration of not being able to play, or the treatment necessary to recover. If you remember that, you can handle any problems."

Several trainers have backgrounds in physical education and have spent many years as high school and college trainers before moving up to the pro ranks. Otho Davis, head trainer with the Philadelphia Eagles, spent 14 years at the college level before coming to the NFL in 1971 with the Baltimore Colts. Eight of those years were at Kent State University, where he received his master's degree in physical

Rhea checks how players feel before a game.

Trainers must watch players for signs of injury.

Helping players to the sideline is a big job.

education. He joined the Eagles in 1973.

Davis says his college experience was "very, very valuable. This is one job you don't start at the pro level. It takes time to learn how to deal with the athletes and the variety of injuries you come across."

During the football season a trainer's work day can be divided into two basic routines: pregame preparations, with the business days normally on Mondays, Wednesdays, and Thursdays; and game day itself—usually Sunday.

On the Monday following a Sunday game, the trainer and his staff give thorough examinations to all players injured the day before. Those with minor or moderate ailments will be given ice, whirlpool treatments, or other therapy designed to

get them ready for practices later in the week and the following Sunday's game. For those who were seriously injured, the trainer and team physician will consult and decide either on medical care or on a rehabilitation program, including weight exercises, which will get the player back into action as soon as possible.

Wednesdays and Thursdays are full practice days for most teams—which means long days for the trainers. Ric McDonald, San Diego's head trainer, says he and his staff begin those days before 8 A.M. and usually don't leave until after 6 P.M. Trainers must work around the practice schedules, so McDonald and his staff get in early to start the whirlpool and other therapy equipment, and begin taping.

Trainers work with doctors to treat injuries.

"We tape right up until the 10:30 meeting," he says, "then work with those players who are out on injured reserve."

Afternoons are taken up with full practice, maybe another meeting, and then removing tape, applying ice and bandages, and dealing with any problems that may have arisen during practice.

On game day, the taping and minor treatment begins early—at around 8:30 or 9 in the morning. That lasts until noon, when the pregame warm-ups begin. Just before the kickoff, the trainers of both teams get together to discuss the location of all sideline emergency equipment. In addition to an ambulance, there are stretchers, oxygen tanks, aspirator, and a defibrillator. The team physician and

trainer are available at all times to respond to any emergencies. San Diego's McDonald says his staff is even aware of the seat locations of a few Chargers fans who are doctors, specializing in neurology and opthalmology, in case there is a head or eye injury with which the regular team physician may need additional assistance.

After the game, the routine is untaping, treatment of assorted minor and moderate injuries, and consultation with physicians on the more serious cases. Sunday's work for the trainers can extend far into the evening.

Atlanta's Rhea says, "Game day can be very, very long, but I enjoy what I do a lot."

AMAZING . . .

Atlanta Falcons nose tackle Wilson Faumuina is the son of a Samoan chieftain.

Chicago Bears wide receiver Brian Baschnagel attended 19 different schools in 12 years. His father was in the military.

The first player to wear glasses in an NFL game was Hall of Fame receiver Raymond Berry, who played for the Baltimore Colts from 1955-1967. He used shaded swimmer's goggles to protect his eyes against the winter sun's glare.

The San Diego Chargers once had two preseason practices on the same day. That's not unusual. What makes this unique is that they had them on fields 3,700 miles apart! It happened during a 1976 trip for games in Tokyo against St. Louis and Honolulu against San Francisco (they lost both). Between the games, the Chargers worked out in Tokyo on Thursday morning, August 19, then left at 7:30 P.M. (Tokyo time). Since they crossed the International Date Line on the flight

across the Pacific Ocean, they arrived in Honolulu at 6:30 A.M. the same day. After a few hours sleep, the Chargers were off to the practice field.

The catering service at the Orange Bowl for Super Bowl XIII ordered the following for sale at concession stands during the game: Four tons of hot dogs, 100 pounds of cheese, 30,000 hamburgers, 100 heads of cabbage for sauerkraut, four tons of ice for drinks, 15,000 gallons of soda, 1,500 pounds of French fries, 15,000 ice cream sandwiches, and 3,000 gallons of coffee.

All goal posts for NFL games must be bright gold in color.

These 12 *men* played in the NFL: Margene Adkins, Vickey Ray Anderson, Gail Cogdill, Blenda Gay, Fair Hooker, June Jones, Dolly King, Tillie Manton, Blanche Martin, Julie Rykovich, Bev Wallace, and Faye Wilson.

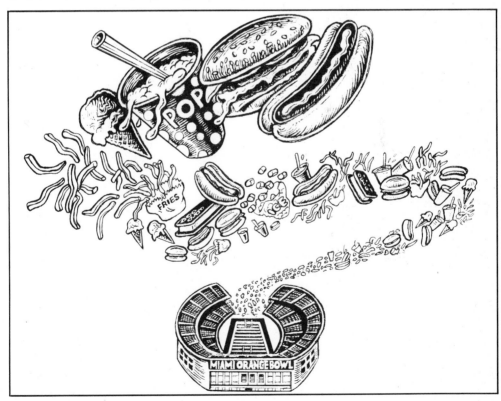

In 1929, Hall of Famer Ernie Nevers scored all 40 of his team's points in a victory over the Chicago Bears. Nevers had six touchdowns and kicked four extra points for the Chicago Cardinals.

Dallas Cowboys linebacker D.D. Lewis's initials stand for Dwight Douglas. He was born shortly after the end of World War II and was named in honor of two American war heroes, Generals Dwight Eisenhower and Douglas MacArthur.

Interstate Highway 75 runs past four NFL stadiums: Detroit's Pontiac Silverdome, Cincinnati's Riverfront Stadium, Atlanta Stadium, and Tampa Stadium.

The Dallas Cowboys have been called "America's Team" and in one sense they are. The Cowboys' games are broadcast over 200 radio stations that cover 17 different states. The broadcasts also are carried by 24 Spanish-speaking stations in five states.

New England Patriots center Bill Lenkaitis is the team's dentist.

Supreme Court Justice Byron (Whizzer) White played in the NFL for the 1938 Pittsburgh Pirates and the 1940-41 Detroit

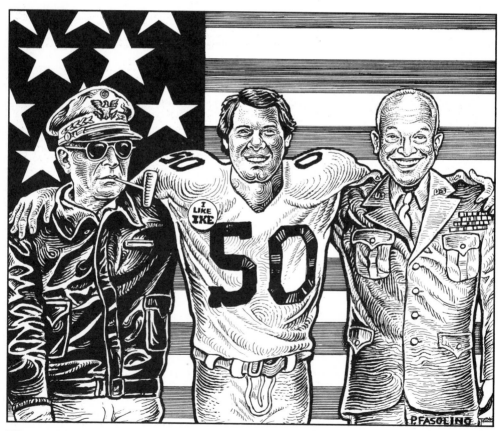

Lions. He led the NFL in rushing in 1938 and 1940. In 1939, he was at Oxford in England as a Rhodes scholar.

An NFL team can play with as few players on the field as it wants, but if the number exceeds 11, it is a penalty.

Houston Oilers kick returner Carl Roaches drove an ice cream truck before making the team in 1980. The man he replaced, Johnnie Dirden, previously drove a cement truck before making the Oilers' roster.

Baltimore Colts quarterback Bert Jones, Kansas City Chiefs guard Brad Budde, and Houston Oilers wide receiver Mike Renfro have something very unique in common. Their fathers all played in the NFL. Dub Jones was a wide receiver for the Cleveland Browns (1950-55), Ed Budde played guard with the Chiefs (1963-1976), and Ray Renfro played wide receiver for the Browns (1952-1963).

Atlanta's wide receiver Alfred Jenkins has a problem: he's very nearsighted. Jenkins wears glasses off the field, but chooses not to use them—or contact lenses—during a game because he believes his condition forces better concentration.

P. FASOLINO

Design Your Own Uniform

Here's your chance to design an NFL uniform. Take a look at the current team uniforms on pages 42 through 56, then try to use colors, stripes, and symbols to create a uniform design of your own.

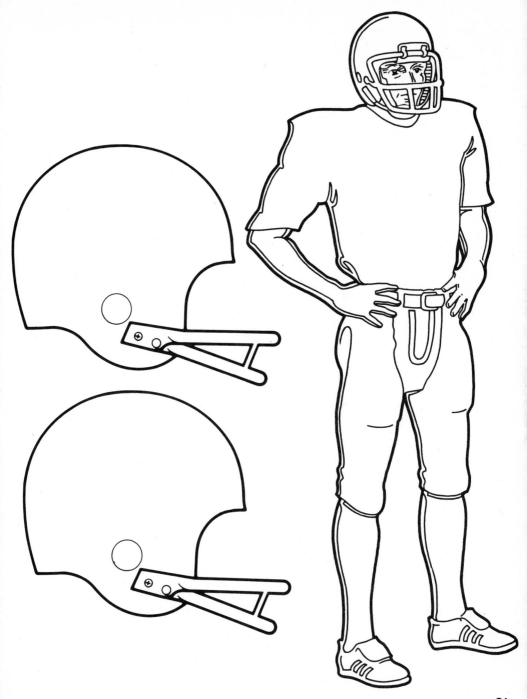

Boys Will Be Boys

NFL players weren't born wearing helmets and shoulder pads. They were kids once, too, and they looked a lot different than they do now. See if you can guess which players the kids here grew up to be. You'll find the answers in the back of the book.

We've Got You Covered

All 28 NFL teams are represented on
the cover of this book. Can you find them all
in the accompanying illustration? The team names
are listed below. Match them up.
The correct answers are on page 96.

AFC	NFC
Baltimore Colts	Atlanta Falcons
Buffalo Bills	Chicago Bears
Cincinnati Bengals	Dallas Cowboys
Cleveland Browns	Detroit Lions
Denver Broncos	Green Bay Packers
Houston Oilers	Los Angeles Rams
Kansas City Chiefs	Minnesota Vikings
Miami Dolphins	New Orleans Saints
New England Patriots	New York Giants
New York Jets	Philadelphia Eagles
Oakland Raiders	St. Louis Cardinals
Pittsburgh Steelers	San Francisco 49ers
San Diego Chargers	Tampa Bay Buccaneers
Seattle Seahawks	Washington Redskins

Editors:
Bill Barron, Jim Natal
Designer:
Glen Iwasaki
Associate Editors:
Larry Eldridge, Chuck Garrity
Production Staff:
Marilyn Arai, Laurel Burden, Jaime Robles, Ken Winikoff
Contributing Writers:
Tony Napoli, Norm Schachter
Editorial Administrative Assistant:
Ellen Galloway

Cover Illustration: *Jack Davis.*
Illustrators: *Merv Corning, 43, 45, 47, 49, 51, 53, 55;*
Jack Davis, 13-19, 87; Peter Fasolino, 76-79;
John Grabowski, 62-63; Dan Hanrahan, 20-21, 68-71, 80-83;
Chuck Ren, 23-27; Richard Tanenbaum, 22; Stevens Wright, 30.

Photographers: *John F. Bard, 36b; Vernon Biever, 5c, 59;*
Bolger/Kanuit, 43abc, 45a, 49bc, 47bc, 51b, 53d, 55d;
David Boss, 60; Buffalo Bills, 9b; Stan Caplan, 57 (I-XIV);
Jim Chaffin, 32c, 33c; Dennis Collins, 8b; Denver Broncos, 5b;
George Gaadt, 6a; George Gellatly, 28; George Gojkovich, 9a;
Pete Groh, 92a; Don Hale, 43d, 45bcd, 47ad, 49ad, 51acd,
53abc, 55abc; Andy Hayt, 4a; Jocelyn Hinsen, 32b, 37a;
Fred Kaplan, 57 (XV); Don Lansu, 92b; Ross Lewis, 31;
Los Angeles Rams, 7a; Ed Mahan, 5a, 88; Al Messerschmidt,
93a; Peter Read Miller, 6b, 38-41; Oakland Raiders, 4b;
Jack O'Grady, 30b; Ron Ross, 36a; Manny Rubio,
66a, 67, 72-75; Bill Smith, 7b; Robert L. Smith, 93; Sue Smith,
32a, 33abd; R.H. Stagg, 7c; Donald J. Stetzer, 37c; Tony
Tomsic, 30a; Herb Weitman, 64, 66b; Hank Young, 92c;
Michael Zagaris, 8a; Howard Zryb, 8c.

ISBN 0-590-31628-1

THE GREAT
NFL FUN BOOK II

SCHOLASTIC BOOK SERVICES
New York Toronto London Auckland Sydney Tokyo